A B C

ROY LICHTENSTEIN'S

abc

Conceived and written by
BOB ADELMAN

Designed by Samuel N. Antupit

A Bulfinch Press Book
Little, Brown and Company
Boston   New York   London

A Bob Adelman Book

First edition
ISBN 0-8212-2591-X
Library of Congress Catalog Card Number: 99-64117
Editor: Mary Beth Brewer
Designer: Samuel N. Antupit
Design Production: Liz Trovato

Bulfinch Press is an imprint and trademark of Little, Brown and Company (Inc.)

Printed in Italy

ACKNOWLEDGMENTS

Visual books are always collaborations.

In a difficult time, Dorothy, David, and Mitchell Lichtenstein's enthusiasm for ABC was heartening.
The managing director of Roy's studio, Cassandra Lozano, ably assisted by Joanna Johnson, led us
cheerfully and expertly through Roy's artistic cornucopia. Shelley Lee nimbly and unflappably
overcame any and all obstacles standing in the book's way.

I would especially like to thank Carol Judy Leslie, the reigning queen of art book publishers,
for immediately saying a delightful three-letter word: Y-E-S!

Sam Antupit, dean of typography and a 26 letterman, graced these pages with his intricate knowledge
and refined sensibilities to typefaces and design. Liz Trovato's formidable skills are displayed on every page.

I am especially indebted to Mary Beth Brewer, bookmaker extraordinaire,
who worked her magic on every aspect of this book from its inception.

Roy's work is replete with words and letters, and he loved good talk. The alphabet is based on type that
he used in his art. Although Roy was with us at the start, ABC has now turned into an homage, alas.

—Bob Adelman

FOR HENRY LICHTENSTEIN AND HARRY REAY
GRAND CHILDREN

ROY LICHTENSTEIN'S
PAINTINGS ARE MADE UP OF
LINES, COLORS, DOTS, STRIPES, AND
SOMETIMES WORDS. TOGETHER THESE
ARE HIS LANGUAGE.

WHEN WE TALK, WRITE, OR READ,
ALL OF US USE WORDS.
WORDS ARE MADE UP OF LETTERS.

ART

Barn   Black   Blue

Cup   Coffee   Curves

Dog   Dots

Explosion   Edges

Flag   Flat   Form

Golf Ball   Goldfish   Grapefruit   Glass   Green

Horses   Hoofs   Heads   Hands

Ice-Cream Soda

J

Jazz

Kiss

Lobster   Lighthouse   Legs   Lines

Mermaid   Model

Nurse   Nose   Neck   Nails

Oval Office

Pyramids　Perspective　Planes　Point

Quack! Quack!

R

RING!

Soda   Straw   Sliced Sandwich

Tears   Throat   Teeth

Uniform

Violin   Violinist

Water Lilies   Water   White

X-in

Yellow

Zipper

LIST OF PLATES

All dimensions are given in inches, height before width.

Page 6
Self Portrait, 1978
Oil and magna on canvas
70 x 54
Private collection

A
Art, 1962
Oil on canvas
36 x 68
Private collection

Look Mickey, 1961
Oil on canvas
48 x 69
National Gallery of Art,
   Washington, D.C.

B
Red Barn II, 1969
Oil and magna on canvas
44 x 56
Museum Ludwig, Cologne, Germany

C
Cup and Saucer II, 1977
Painted and patinated bronze
Sculpture: 43 3/4 x 25 3/4 x 10;
   base: 20 x 12 x 27; edition of 3
   and maquette
Private collection

D
Grrrrrrrrrrrr!!, 1965
Oil and magna on canvas
68 x 56
Solomon R. Guggenheim Museum,
   New York

E
Explosion, 1965
Oil and magna on canvas
56 x 48
Private collection

F
Forms in Space, 1985
Screenprint on Rives BFK paper
Sheet: 35 3/4 x 52;
   Image: 31 1/8 x 42 1/2
Edition: 125
Private collection

G
*Still Life with Goldfish (and
   Painting of Golf Ball)*, 1972
Oil and magna on canvas
52 x 42
Private collection

H
The Red Horseman, 1974
Oil and magna on canvas
84 x 112
Ludwig Collection, Museum
Moderner Kunst, Vienna, Austria

I
Ice Cream Soda, 1962
Oil on canvas
64 x 32
Private collection

J
Aspen Winter Jazz Poster, 1967
Screenprint on heavy, glossy
   white paper
Sheet: 40 x 26; Image: 40 x 26
Edition: 300
Private collection

K
Kiss II, 1962
Oil on canvas
57 x 68
Private collection

L
Cape Cod Still Life II, 1973
Oil and magna on canvas
60 x 74
Private collection

M

Mermaid (sculpture maquette), 1978
Painted wood
59 1/4 x 70 3/4 x 34
Private collection

N

Nurse, 1964
Oil and magna on canvas
48 x 48
Private collection

O

Oval Office, 1993
Oil and magna on canvas
126 x 161
Private collection

P

Study for "The Great Pyramid," 1969
Oil and magna on canvas
43 x 68
Private collection

Q

Reflections: Portrait of a Duck, 1989
Oil and magna on canvas
50 1/8 x 60 1/8
Private collection

R

-R-R-R-R-Ring!!, 1962
Oil on canvas
24 x 16
Private collection

S

Sandwich and Soda, 1964
Screenprint on clear plastic
Sheet: 20 x 24; Image: 19 x 23
Edition: 500
Private collection

T

Frightened Girl, 1964
Oil on canvas
48 x 48
Private collection

U

Mr. Bellamy, 1961
Oil on canvas
56 1/2 x 42 1/2
Modern Art Museum of Fort
   Worth, Texas

V

Salzburger Festspiele 1991
   (collage for poster), 1991
Painted and printed paper on board
21 1/4 x 28 3/16
Private collection

W

Les Nymphéas
   (collage for print), 1992
Painted and printed board on paper
26 1/4 x 35 7/8
Private collection

X

Desk Calendar, 1962
Oil on canvas
48 1/2 x 68 1/4
Museum of Contemporary Art,
   Los Angeles, Panza Collection

Y

Yellow Brushstroke I, 1965
Oil on canvas
68 1/8 x 55 7/8
Kunsthaus, Zurich, Switzerland

Z

Zipper, 1962
Graphite on paper
Sheet: 22 1/2 x 19 3/4;
   Image 15 x 14 1/2
Private collection

A

B C

D ! E F G

H I J K L M

N O P Q R S

T U V W X Y Z

Art books are usually printed in a combination of standard colors.
Here, however, we have matched the colors to actual paint chips from
Lichtenstein's palette. Thus red, blue, yellow, green, and black as they
appear on the page duplicate as closely as possible
the colors found in the original art.

Each of the alphabet letters has been drawn by hand, but all are
based on letters that appear in Lichtenstein's art. The letters J, W,
and Z are based on the typeface Futura. L, N, and U are from Radiant,
the face used in Lichtenstein's posters for Lincoln Center's jazz
festival and for the Guthrie Theatre's *Merton of the Movies*. B and T
are done in Stencil, the face used on his 1993 CARE poster.
E comes from an early lithograph, *Ten Dollar Bill,* and K and S are
based on comic-strip lettering. F and M originate from the word
FORM, part of his mural *Large Interior with Three Reflections.*
In a few cases, the letters are reproduced directly from the works
illustrated: For example, R is from *-R-R-R-R-Ring!!*

The text of the book is set in Tekton Oblique inspired by
comic-strip lettering. Tekton is an Adobe Originals typeface
designed by David Siegel in 1989.